JOURNEY THROUGH

ANCIENT CIVILIZATIONS

ROGER COOTE

HAMLYN

THE FIRST HUMANS

Around 10 million years ago the climate in Africa was changing, and areas of thick forest were being replaced by grasslands. The apes that lived in the forest trees began spending more of their time on the ground, searching for plants to eat. Gradually they learned to stand and walk on two legs, which meant they could use their hands for other things, including gathering food.

Over millions of years, the apes evolved into what are called hominids - human-like creatures. The earliest hominids, now known as australopithecines, appeared around 4 million years ago in East and southern Africa. Archaeologists have found fossil footprints, preserved in hardened volcanic ash, which show that australopithecines walked upright. They have also discovered parts of the skeleton of a female, nicknamed Lucy, who lived 3.4 million years ago in what is now Ethiopia.

Toolmakers

There were four different species of australopithecines. By about 2 million years ago one species had developed into a creature called *Homo*, which had a larger brain than its ancestors and a more human-looking face. The earliest *Homo* species differed from the australopithecines in another, important way: it could make tools such as axes and scrapers by chipping flakes from stones to make a sharp edge. For this reason it has been christened *Homo habilis*, or "handy man".

The *Homo habilis* species may have used their tools for hunting animals, but it is more likely that they used them simply for cutting and scraping meat from carcasses that they found. Their major source of food was still plants, nuts, and berries. It is thought that they built small huts to shelter in - the first buildings in the world.

Hunter Gatherers and Modern Humans

Around 1.7 million years ago *Homo habilis* evolved into *Homo erectus*, the first hominid to hunt animals for food. At first they killed small creatures, such as bushpigs and hares, but as they learned to hunt in groups they tackled larger prey, including giant baboons. Meat was not their only food: they also ate various different types of plant, including roots that they dug from the earth.

The *Homo erectus* species were the first people to venture from Africa to Europe and Asia. As they moved northwards they had to adapt to living in the colder climates they found. This was possible partly because they had discovered how to make fire by rubbing sticks together, and so could keep warm. Fire also enabled them to cook meat and keep dangerous wild animals away.

A new species, *Homo sapiens neanderthalensis*, which was very like modern humans, evolved from *Homo erectus* between 200,000 and 150,000 years ago. Groups of Neanderthals lived in Europe, parts of the Middle East, and what is now the southern USSR. Although they are often thought of as primitive cave men, they were much more intelligent than their ancestors and could make better tools. They also seem to have looked after old and sick members of their group, even though these people would not have been able to take part in hunting. Some Neanderthals lived in huts built from animal skins and the bones of mammoths - huge elephant-like creatures that were hunted for food.

Truly modern humans, *Homo sapiens sapiens*, first appeared in Africa about 100,000 years ago. They moved on into Europe and replaced other human species, including the Neanderthals, around 35,000 years ago. Modern humans also reached Australia from Asia 50,000 years ago and North America from Asia about 40,000 years ago.

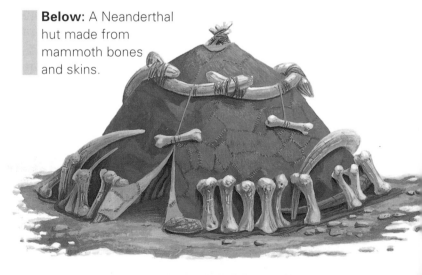

Below: A Neanderthal hut made from mammoth bones and skins.

Below: By hunting in groups and using clubs as weapons, *Homo erectus* was able to kill large animals such as baboons.

THE DEVELOPMENT OF MODERN HUMANS

Our evolution from hominids (australopithecus) to modern humans (*Homo sapiens*) took 4 million years. Each new creature that evolved had a larger brain than the one before.

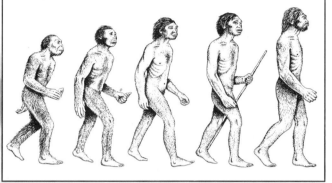

NEANDERTHALS c.200,000 YEARS AGO • FIRST MODERN HUMANS 100,000 YEARS AGO

THE FIRST FARMERS

Around 12,000 years ago, important changes began to happen in an area known as the Fertile Crescent - what we now call Turkey, Israel, Iraq, and Iran. The climate was becoming warmer and more moist, and this helped wild plants - especially grasses - to grow in abundance. The hunter gatherers who lived there discovered that the seeds of these grasses were good to eat, and they began harvesting them with flint-bladed knives. Gradually they learned to produce more food by planting the grass seeds themselves. They planted the best seeds they could find and so their crops slowly improved until they became

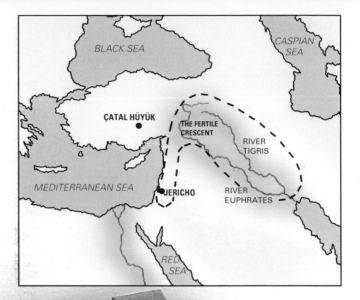

Below: The farming village of Çatal Hüyük covered an area of 13 hectares.

Right: The Fertile Crescent, where agriculture first began around 12,000 years ago.

in one place, and this meant they could build permanent homes to live in. The farmers made their homes close together and built walls around their settlements to protect themselves from attackers. These were the first settled communities in the world.

Jericho

Around 9,500 years ago a group of farmers settled at a site called Jericho in the Fertile Crescent. With its rich soil and a spring to provide water, the area was ideal for growing wheat and barley and for keeping sheep and goats. The farmers built themselves huts using bricks made from dried mud, and constructed a strong stone wall, 3 m thick and 4 m high, around the settlement.

As more and more food was grown, the number of people who could be fed increased and the community grew. At one stage Jericho may have been home to as many as 2,000 people. Being able to grow more food also meant that not everyone had to work in the fields. Some people became specialized craftsmen, making tools, jewellery, and clay pots to store and cook food in.

Çatal Hüyük

The village of Çatal Hüyük, in what is now Turkey, was founded around 7,000 years ago. Like Jericho, it was surrounded by good farmland and it grew rapidly in size. The inhabitants became very wealthy by trading with other settlements. Nearby was a source of obsidian, a type of natural glass found in volcanic rocks and used for making tools and ornaments. This was exchanged for other goods such as timber, copper, and even cowrie shells from as far away as the Red Sea. The craftsmen of Çatal Hüyük became very skilled at making copper jewellery, textiles, obsidian arrowheads and daggers, and carved stone figures. They also found out how to make bronze - a mixture of copper and tin - and tools made from bronze gradually replaced stone ones.

The people of Jericho had probably worshipped their ancestors. In Çatal Hüyük religion became an increasingly important part of life. We do not know exactly what people believed in, although they may have worshipped bulls in specially built shrines. We do know that a group of priests and priestesses developed and became very powerful there.

Above: This statue was made in Jericho over 8,000 years ago. The eyes are made from shells.

like the cereals we know today - barley, wheat, and rye. These first farmers also started to keep animals, such as sheep and goats, for meat and milk.

People in other places were learning how to farm, too. Yams were grown in South-East Asia around 9,000 years ago, and cereal crops were first cultivated in China and Central America more than 7,000 years ago.

The hunter gatherers of the past had moved from place to place, searching for new supplies of food. When people began farming they were able to settle

ANCIENT EGYPT

Around 5000 BC, farmers began to cultivate the rich soil which lay in a narrow strip on either side of the River Nile in Egypt and at the delta where the river flowed into the sea. This fertile soil was left behind when the river flooded each year. The land on either side was dry, barren desert, and without the Nile there would have been no early civilization in Egypt.

The population increased quickly and farming villages grew in size. The first walled cities appeared at Naqada and Hieraconopolis in about 3300 BC, near the tombs of dead rulers. In 3100 BC Egypt became a unified state ruled by kings, called pharaohs, with their capital at Memphis.

The Ancient Egyptians believed in life after death, and the tombs of kings and other rich people were filled with things that the dead person would need in the afterlife, including cooking pots and jewellery. Stone carvings and paintings decorated the walls. The body was buried in a pit and then covered with sand, which dried out the corpse and preserved it. It was believed that the person's spirit would then be able to recognize it and return to it in the afterlife. A flat-topped structure, called a mastaba, was built over the pit using mud bricks.

The Pyramids

In about 2700 BC, at the start of what is called the Old Kingdom, the Egyptians began to build a new type of tomb for their pharaohs. A stone pyramid was constructed at Saqqara, near Memphis, for the pharaoh Zoser. It had four sides that rose up in steps to a height of 62 m and was the largest structure the world had ever seen.

The Egyptians now began to prepare some bodies for the afterlife in a new way. When an important person died, his or her body was preserved by mummification. The person's insides were removed and the body was soaked in a special preserving fluid. It was then dried, wrapped in bandages and buried inside several coffins in a deep tomb. Mummified bodies could remain well preserved for many centuries.

Soon after this even bigger pyramids were built, with smooth sides instead of steps. The Great Pyramid of King Khufu, built at Giza in about 2450 BC, is 147 m high. It is thought to contain 2.3 million stone blocks, each weighing about 2.5 tonnes. Around the huge

Above: This Egyptian hieroglyphic writing from Saqqara is about 4,500 years old.

Below: The Great Pyramid at Giza, where King Khufu was buried around 2,450 BC.

pyramid are smaller ones built for Khufu's queens, mastabas for the bodies of the king's relatives and officials, and pits containing dismantled boats for use in the afterlife.

Work on building the pyramids and the "cities of the dead" that surrounded them was carried out from July to October each year. At that time, farmers could not cultivate their crops because the Nile was in flood and the fields were under water.

The End of the Old Kingdom

Ancient Egypt was governed by a group of ministers who were responsible to the king. The chief minister, or vizier, was in charge of administration, justice, and taxation. The country was divided into provinces, each ruled by a governor. By 2400 BC, these governors had become extremely powerful and the pharaoh was unable to control them. They built up their own armies and raised taxes for themselves rather than for the pharaoh. But the final blow to the Old

Kingdom was caused by the very thing upon which life in Egypt depended - the Nile.

The annual flooding of the river was never very predictable, and in some years the water did not rise high enough to cover all the fields. Around 2150 BC, there were several years of very low flooding. This greatly reduced the amount of food that could be grown and caused terrible famines which destroyed the power of the kingdom.

Below: Egypt during the old kingdom, which began in 2700 BC.

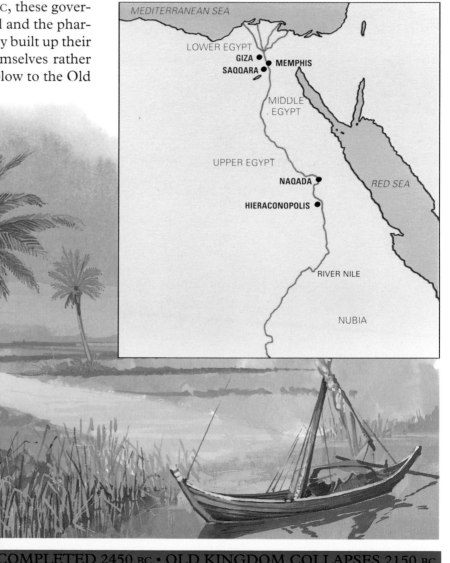

THE INDUS VALLEY

As had happened both in Egypt and Mesopotamia, the first great civilization in India grew up around a river - the Indus. The first cities developed around 2500 BC on a broad plain in the north-west of the subcontinent, with the Thar Desert on one side and the highlands of Baluchistan on the other. Like the Nile, the Indus floods each year and when the floodwaters recede they leave behind a layer of fertile silt over a large area. The Indus Valley civilization was able to develop because of this rich soil, on which barley and wheat could be grown without irrigation.

About 100 Indus settlements have been found dating from between 2500 and 2000 BC, and most of them were quite sizeable towns surrounded by defensive walls of baked brick. The cities of the Indus Valley were the first places in the world where iron was produced by heating the iron ore that is found in rocks, a process called smelting. A form of writing was also invented there at approximately the same time.

As well as supporting their populations by growing crops, the towns seem to have traded with each other and with other civilizations. Archaeologists have found Indus seals - used for securing bales of merchandise - at sites in Mesopotamia, and some Mesopotamian goods in the Indus city of Mohenjo-daro. Much of this trade went by sea, although there were also overland trade routes to Afghanistan and Persia. Goods were probably carried along these land routes in bullock-carts, as clay models of carts

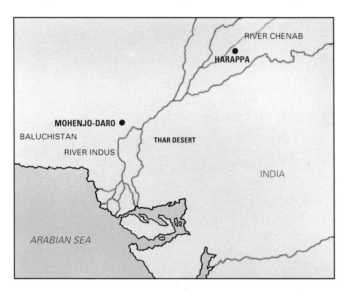

RIVER CHENAB
HARAPPA
MOHENJO-DARO
BALUCHISTAN
RIVER INDUS
THAR DESERT
INDIA
ARABIAN SEA

Left: The first towns and cities in India grew up along the fertile valley of the River Indus. The largest were Harappa and Mohenjo-daro.

Below: The walled citadel of an Indus valley city was surrounded by houses and rich agricultural land.

FIRST CITIES IN INDUS VALLEY c.2500 BC • WHEAT AND BARLEY MAIN CROPS GROWN

Right: A seal used by merchants and a clay model of a bullock-cart from Mohenjo-daro.

have been found in a number of Indus towns and cities. The goods that were exported included cotton cloth - the first of its kind in the world - pottery, bead necklaces, and skilfully crafted shells and metalwork.

Mohenjo-daro and Harappa

The two largest cities of the Indus Valley were Mohenjo-daro, near to the point where the Indus flowed into the Arabian Sea, and Harappa, which was further upstream on a tributary of the Indus called the River Chenab.

Each of these two cities covered an area of about 60 hectares and may have housed 40,000 people. In the centre of both cities was an artificial mound, called a citadel, on which religious and government buildings were constructed. There was also a large granary where grain was stored so that there was enough to last all through the year.

The citadel overlooked the surrounding streets and houses. The streets were carefully planned, with rows of houses crossing at right-angles and a system of sewers and drains. The larger houses consisted of a number of rooms built around an open courtyard. Some houses had bathrooms and toilets. The courtyard often had a brick-lined shaft in the floor, which may have been a well or a place to store jars and vases. Stairs in the courtyard led to the upper storey of the house or to a flat roof. Poorer people lived in houses with only one room.

Sudden Collapse

The Indus Valley civilization was well organized. The weights made for weighing goods were the same everywhere, as was the writing that was used, and in Mohenjo-daro and other cities the buildings were all constructed from bricks of the same standard size. Yet the civilization seems to have ended suddenly in about 1500 BC. We do not know for certain why this happened. Mohenjo-daro probably declined when the River Indus changed its course, which meant that the surrounding fields were not fertilized when it flooded and so did not produce enough crops. Other towns were attacked by invaders from the north. What we do know is that the great towns and cities of the Indus Valley crumbled and were replaced by small farming villages.

FIRST EVER COTTON TEXTILES MADE • CIVILIZATION ENDS SUDDENLY c.1500 BC

SHANG CHINA

Left: The first great civilization in China - the Shang - began around the Yellow River.

Below: An oracle bone with Chinese writing carved on it.

Bottom: These workmen are building a rammed-earth wall to protect their city.

The world's fourth great civilization - after Sumer, Egypt, and the Indus Valley - grew up in north-east China. From about 4000 BC there were farming communities around the Yellow River and the River Yangtze. At first the people lived in temporary settlements, and survived by hunting, fishing, and growing a few crops before moving on to another site. Later they built larger, permanent villages and spent more of their time on agriculture.

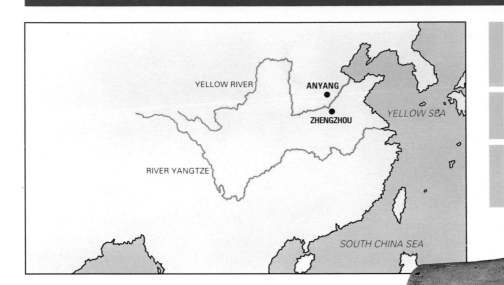

FARMING VILLAGES NEAR YELLOW RIVER c.4000 BC • SHANG DYNASTY c.1800 BC

The early Chinese farmers depended on the rivers for water to grow their crops of millet, cabbages, and plums. They also used them for transport. But the presence of the rivers also had major disadvantages - especially the floods that occasionally covered vast areas and drowned thousands of people.

The First Dynasty

Between about 2500 and 1800 BC, during what is called the Longshan period, walled towns were built and crafts such as metal-working and pottery-making developed in China. Around 1800 BC China's first dynasty, or ruling family, appeared at the start of the major civilization which has been named after them - the Shang.

The centre of Shang China was on the western edge of the North China Plain. This is the area in which the Yellow River flows from the mountains to the north and drops its load of fertile silt. The fertile area extended east towards the Yellow Sea and south towards the River Yangtze. The main crop grown on the plain was millet, although in the east, rice was cultivated in paddy-fields watered by the river. The northern mountains provided rich supplies of metals, including copper, tin, and gold. Shang craftsmen made weapons and beautiful ceremonial vases from bronze, and they were also skilled at painting with lacquer, and carving stone and jade.

One of the earliest Shang capitals was at Zhengzhou, near the south of the fertile plain. It was founded in about 1700 BC. At its centre was a raised platform of earth, more than 7 km long and over 9 m high, which was surrounded by a wall. On the platform were the palace buildings of the ruling family, and outside the city walls were workshops and the houses where the ordinary citizens lived.

The Shang seem to have moved their capital city several times, possibly because of flooding or invasions by enemies. About 1400 BC Anyang became the capital. Around this city are graves, some of which are thought to contain the last of the Shang kings. Although these graves were robbed centuries ago, some of the items that remain - including bronze objects, jade and bone carvings, and cowrie shells that were used as money - suggest that they once contained treasures of immense value.

Religion and Warfare

Religion played an important role in Shang China. People worshipped their ancestors in their own homes and asked for their guidance on future events. They also heated bones - especially the shoulder blades of cattle - to make them crack, and then "read" the shapes of the cracks to tell fortunes. The earliest form of Chinese writing, dating from about 1400 BC, was found carved on these so-called "oracle bones".

The Shang were always threatened by attackers from the north and west, and warfare was a central part of their society. War chariots and bronze weapons were sometimes buried with dead nobles. Eventually the Shang dynasty came to an end during the eleventh century BC, when nomads from the west invaded and established the Chou dynasty.

Below: A bronze vessel in the shape of a tiger protecting a man.

IMPERIAL EGYPT

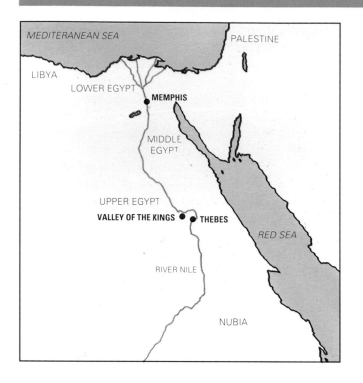

Above: Egypt at the time of the New Kingdom.

Egypt's Old Kingdom ended in about 2150 BC (see pages 12-13) and was followed by a period in which the country broke down into a network of provinces, each ruled by its own governor. In around 2040 BC Egypt's pharaohs managed to reunite the land and the era known as the Middle Kingdom began.

The Middle Kingdom

Life in the Middle Kingdom continued much as it had done in the days of the Old Kingdom. Agriculture was totally dependent upon the Nile. The river flooded every July to October and crops were planted between November and February. Paintings inside tombs show farmers ploughing their land, sowing crops and harvesting wheat, barley, vegetables, lentils, and fruit. Despite the vital part they played in supplying Egypt with food, farmers were looked down upon by others. Priests, viziers, scribes, merchants, and craftsmen were all regarded as far superior to those who fed them.

The priests' duties involved serving in the temples which were built to honour Egypt's many gods and goddesses. Each *nome*, or administrative region, had its own god, and there were many others as well, including the sun god Ra, the moon god Thoth, Osiris, the god of the Underworld, and Anubis, the god of mummification. The pharaoh was thought to be a god himself - the living embodiment of the falcon-headed god Horus.

The viziers were very powerful because they were the pharaohs' advisers and supervised the royal court. Scribes also had an important job - overseeing the harvest and writing down how much of each crop had been produced. They also recorded the history of their times. Egyptian hieroglyphic writing was first used in about 3000 BC, and at that time scribes wrote on clay tablets. About 400 years later, however, papyrus - a form of paper made from flattened reeds - was invented.

Craftsmen in cities and villages throughout Egypt produced beautiful metalwork, furniture, pottery, jewellery, and fabrics. These items were made both for use within Egypt and for export to other lands. The most skilful craftsmen were employed in the royal workshops, where they spent their time making furnishings for the pharaohs' tombs.

The New Kingdom

During the Middle Kingdom the provinces once again started to become independent and power slipped away from the pharaohs around 1783 BC. By 1570 BC they had regained their hold on the country and the New Kingdom began, with its centre in the city of Thebes.

Between 1570 and 1080 BC Egypt reached the height of its wealth and power. Nubia, to the south, was seized, with its rich deposits of gold, and Syria and Palestine were also conquered. The craftsmen of the New Kingdom produced even finer work than before, as can be seen from the superb items found in the tomb of the pharaoh Tutankhamun.

When pharaohs died they were no longer buried in pyramids. Despite being carefully sealed to deter robbers, most pyramids had already been plundered of their treasures. The New Kingdom pharaohs decided to make their tombs less obvious by hiding them in a small valley across the river from Thebes - the Valley of the Kings. There they were buried,

MIDDLE KINGDOM c.2040-1783 BC • NEW KINGDOM 1570-1080 BC

Right and below:
Treasures from
Tutankhamun's grave in
the Valley of the Kings.

with all the beautiful objects they would need in their life after death, in deep tombs cut out of the rock. Not even these precautions could protect them from the grave-robbers, however, and only Tutankhamun's tomb remained undiscovered for long.

As had happened at the end of the Old Kingdom, there was a period in the twelfth century BC during which the flooding of the Nile became very unpredictable and famine swept through Egypt. The price of grain rose dramatically and riots broke out. To add to this, the country was attacked by land and sea during the reign of Rameses III (1198-1166 BC), the last great pharaoh. On land, the threat came from the Libyans to the west, on the sea from the "Sea Peoples", who came from various parts of the eastern Mediterranean. By 935 BC Egypt was ruled by kings from Libya.

Below: A funeral
procession in the
Valley of the Kings,
across the Nile from
the city of Thebes.

PEOPLE OF THE STEPPES

The grasslands of the Steppes stretch right across Asia from Manchuria in the far north of China to the Ukraine in the south-eastern USSR. Although some parts of this vast area were inhabited between 5000 and 4000 BC, others were too dry to be used for growing crops. However after 2000 BC nomadic cultures grew up, and a thousand years later most of the Steppes were occupied.

Nomadic Life

There are very few remains of the Steppe civilizations. This is mainly because of their nomadic way of life, which involved moving constantly from place to place in search of new grazing land for their herds of cattle, sheep, and horses. The people never stopped for long in one area and so they did not build permanent houses; instead they lived in tents which could be packed away and carried to the next site. Some permanent settlements were built, but these were mainly at the western edge of the Steppes near the Black Sea.

The most lasting evidence left by the nomads was in the form of burial mounds, called barrows. In some barrows, especially those of the Scythian people of southern Russia, rich treasures have been found, including gold weapons and jewellery, and silver vases for holding wine and oil. Some of the burial gifts made to dead Scythian chiefs were the work of local craftsmen, while others were produced by Greek artists. In the same way, Scythian art frequently showed local animals, including horses, yak, lions, and wild boar, but other creatures not to be found in the surrounding area were also portrayed. We can therefore be sure that the Scythians came into contact with other civilizations.

Besides wearing jewellery, some nomadic people also decorated their bodies. The corpse of one chief, found at Pazyryk in Mongolia, had large tattoos on its skin. The people also changed the shape of their heads by binding babies' skulls tightly, forcing them to become extended as they grew.

Horse-riding spread through the Steppes after 2000 BC, and barrows often contain the skeletons of horses which were sacrificed when a chief died. Humans - probably the chief's servants - were also killed and buried with him in the barrow. Warfare

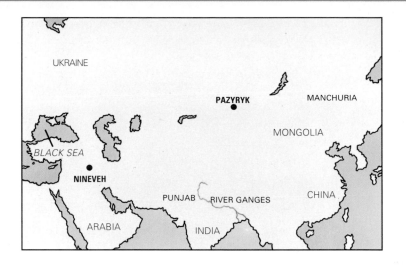

Above: Most of the vast area of the Steppes was occupied by 1000 BC.

Below: Steppe nomads moving a herd of horses to new grazing land.

was common between the various nomadic groups; the warriors fought on horseback using bows, swords, and long lances.

Scythians in Mesopotamia and India

During the seventh century BC, the Scythians began to play a part in the affairs of areas to the south of their lands. They occupied the mountains that formed the northern border of the Assyrian empire and then joined with the Medes and Babylonians to attack Assyria. They captured the Assyrians' cities one by one and finally overran the capital, Nineveh, in 612 BC. Later, the Persian empire led by Darius I attempted to conquer the Scythians. However, the nomads crushed his army in battle on the plains of southern Russia and Darius was forced back.

The Scythians remained unconquered until Philip of Macedon subdued them between 354 and 339 BC. Even then Scythian power continued further east. One Scythian tribe moved down into India around 200 BC and occupied the Punjab and part of the River Ganges valley. It was later forced out and driven westwards towards the Parthian empire. The Scythians caused the Parthians great problems and killed two of their kings in battle, but eventually they were absorbed into the Parthian empire.

Above: A wall hanging from a burial mound at Pazyryk showing a Steppe horseman.

OCEANIA

The first people arrived in Australia between 70,000 and 50,000 years ago. They sailed across the sea from South-East Asia and settled around the coasts of their new land. It must have been difficult for them to adapt, as they found new plants and animals that were very different from those in their homeland.

Around 7,000 years ago, the level of the sea began to rise and the early Australians moved inland. They remained hunter gatherers and fishers, and did not discover how to grow crops or herd livestock until Europeans arrived in the eighteenth century AD.

Melanesia

The small islands which make up Melanesia, to the north-east of Australia, were colonized much later than Australia itself. The first settlers sailed there from eastern Indonesia about 4,000 years ago, taking with them many of the things they needed to start a new life, including crop plants and animals. They also took their distinctive pottery, known as *Lapita*, which was very finely decorated.

The Melanesians were skilful boat-builders; their sail-driven canoes had to be large and strong to carry them and their supplies on such a long voyage. The canoes' hulls were probably built from hollowed-out tree trunks. Each canoe consisted of two hulls, fixed beneath a row of curved timber supports. Passengers and cargo were carried on a platform which was tied on top of the supports. The largest canoes were over 30 m long.

These early mariners must have been good navigators, too, as the tiny Melanesian islands are in the world's largest ocean, the Pacific. They steered their course by watching the positions of the stars and the Sun, and by studying the direction of the wind. They made navigation charts in the form of a framework of wooden strips on which cowrie shells were fixed to mark the position of islands (see top right). Some of the wooden strips showed places where there were strong ocean currents.

The Polynesian Islands

In about 1300 BC, settlers reached the island of Fiji, at the eastern edge of Melanesia. Soon after, they sailed further east into what is called Polynesia. They arrived in Tonga and Samoa around 1100 BC and

Right: A Polynesian voyager and a twin hulled canoe.

Below: Nearly all of Polynesia was settled by AD 1000.

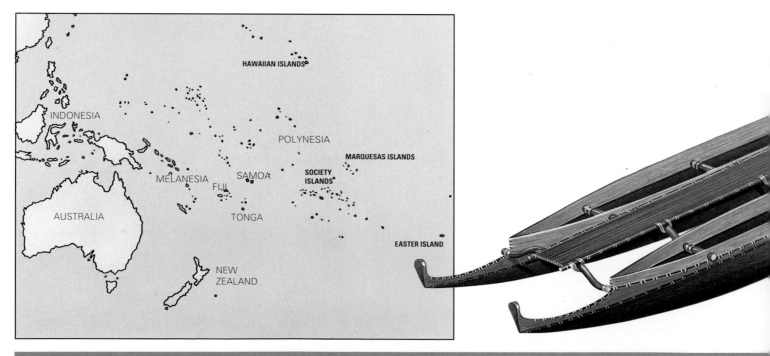

remained there for more than a thousand years, isolated from the rest of the world.

The people of Polynesia lived by fishing, growing crops such as yams, taro (a tropical plant with large, edible roots), coconuts, breadfruit, and bananas, and raising pigs and poultry. As well as their *Lapita* pottery, they made ornaments and tools from shells, obsidian, and stone.

In around 200 BC, people from Samoa sailed their canoes to the east and settled in the Marquesas Islands. These islands became the centre from which the rest of Polynesia was colonized. Canoes carrying settlers with their plants, animals, fishing equipment, and ornaments sailed from the Marquesas to the Hawaiian Islands in AD 400. By 800 Easter Island and the Society Islands had been colonized, and in around 900 people reached New Zealand.

By about AD 1000, almost every island in Polynesia had been visited and most of them had permanent settlements. Wherever they settled, the Polynesian people introduced new crops, animals, and farming methods. Their achievement is amazing because of the vast area in which their settlements are found; some of their sea voyages, made in open canoes, covered up to 4,000 km.

Below: An early Aboriginal rock painting from Australia.

SETTLERS SPREAD FROM MARQUESAS THROUGHOUT POLYNESIA c. AD 300-1000

MINOAN CRETE

Left: This fresco showing leaping dolphins decorated the wall of the Queen's Room in the palace at Knossos.

Below: Minoans in the main courtyard at Knossos.
Inset: The palace itself.

START OF MINOAN CIVILIZATION c.2000 BC • GREAT PALACES BUILT 2000-1700 BC

The Minoan civilization developed on the Mediterranean island of Crete, to the south of Greece. People first settled there in about 6000 BC, and gradually small settlements and then larger towns appeared. According to legend, Crete was ruled by King Minos, who controlled the Aegean Sea with his powerful navy. We cannot be certain that Minos ever really existed, but he gave his name to Europe's first major civilization.

Between 2000 and 1700 BC a number of states grew up in Crete. They were established around the most important cities - Knossos, Phaistos, Mallia, and Zakro. These cities, which all had royal palaces at their centre, were joined by a network of roads.

The Palace of Knossos

The largest and grandest of the Minoan palaces was at Knossos. The first palace there, built in 2000 BC, was destroyed by an earthquake and then built once again in 1700 BC. Ceremonial rooms and royal apartments were arranged around a central courtyard. The walls of the apartments were decorated with beautiful frescoes (made by painting on to wet plaster) showing fish and dolphins, court rituals, and sports. Beneath the apartments were storerooms filled with grain, wine, and olive oil. This produce was collected from the neighbouring fields and redistributed to the people in the city and the nearby towns. The palace also had its own workshops,

where craftsmen worked gold, bronze, copper, gemstones, and ivory. Minoan potters were especially skilful, and produced finely decorated vases and pots for export to Egypt, Cyprus, and the Levant.

To one side of the palace was a second courtyard, which may have been used for spectator sports. One of the most popular sports was bull-leaping, which is depicted in Minoan frescoes. The aim was to somersault over a bull as it charged, avoiding its long, sharp horns. In the frescoes, men are painted red and women white - a tradition that was used in Egypt at the same time.

Writing was another import from Egypt. Hieroglyphics were probably brought to Crete in around 1900 BC, although the Minoans later developed their own style of writing - known as "Linear A". Examples of another script, "Linear B", have also been found in Crete, but it is probable that this was introduced by the Mycenaeans of mainland Greece (see pages 30-31). Writing was needed for keeping records of the goods passing into and out of palaces.

Minoan Gods

Unlike other civilizations at the time, the Minoans did not build temples to their gods. Instead, they worshipped in sacred caves in the mountains and in hill-top sanctuaries. They believed in a number of gods, although we do not know for certain what they were. The double-headed axe was a sacred emblem which probably symbolized a particular god; a gold axe dating from 1500 BC was found in the sacred cave at Arkalochri, south-east of Knossos. Minoan deities may have included a god of animals, a goddess of hunting, and a great Earth mother. Small shrines were built in ordinary homes, mostly to honour the snake goddess who was regarded as the guardian spirit of the house.

The Minoan civilization came to a sudden end in about 1450 BC. The reason may have been a huge volcanic eruption on the island of Thera, 130 km to the north, causing earthquakes and a tidal wave which destroyed the cities and their palaces. It is more likely, however, that the island, already weakened by natural disasters, was attacked by people from mainland Greece. Knossos was later rebuilt, but under new rulers - the Mycenaean Greeks.

THE BABYLONIANS

There was probably a settlement at Babylon from around 3000 BC but it did not develop into a city until after 2500 BC. It grew thanks to its position on the River Euphrates, which was an important trade route linking the Arabian Gulf to northern Mesopotamia, Syria, Anatolia, and the cities of the eastern Mediterranean coast.

By about 2000 BC, when the Sumerian civilization was losing strength, Babylon had become the most powerful kingdom in southern Mesopotamia. It took advantage of Sumer's weakness and swept in, overpowering the old city-states. Marduk, the god worshipped in Babylon, became the most important deity in the newly-founded empire of Babylonia.

The Reign of Hammurabi

Under Hammurabi, who ruled from about 1792 to 1750 BC, Babylonian civilization reached its peak. The knowledge and myths of the Sumerians were absorbed and improved; mathematics, in particular, advanced rapidly. Perhaps the most impressive achievement, however, was the work of Hammurabi himself. He devised a long code of laws, numbering about 200 in all, covering the three classes of Babylonian society - nobles, common people, and slaves. The punishments which were handed out to those who broke the law depended upon which class the offender belonged to. For example, if a noble broke another noble's bone, the aggressor was to have one of his bones broken; if he broke a commoner's bone he paid his victim one unit of silver; and if he broke a slave's bone he paid the slave's master half of the value of the slave. Many of Hammurabi's laws governed everyday matters of trade, agriculture, and wages. However, the written records of the time show that they were not always obeyed.

The Defeat of Babylon

Throughout his reign, Hammurabi tried to make southern Mesopotamia a permanent, unified kingdom under the control of Babylon. He kept a very

Left: This terracotta figure of a lion-headed monster portrayed the Babylonian god Marduk.

Below: The Ishtar Gate at Babylon was built during the reign of King Nebuchadnezzar.

RISE OF BABYLONIA BEGINS 2000 BC • CIVILIZATION AT ITS PEAK 1792-1750 BC

tight grip on the running of Babylonia; many of his "letters", written on clay tablets, have survived and they show how determined he was to make sure that the administration of the empire ran smoothly. When he died there was no one who could take over this massive task, and Babylonia fell to pieces.

For the next 150 years, Babylonia was in something of a backwater, isolated from the great events taking place around it. Meanwhile the Hittites (see pages 28-29) grew in power; in 1595 BC the Hittite ruler Mursilis I launched a devastating raid on Babylon. The city later became part of the Assyrian empire, though only for a short time. In about 1200 BC, Babylon was captured by the Cassites from the Zagros mountains to the east, and ruled by them for more than 400 years. Late in the eighth century BC southern Mesopotamia came under the control of the Chaldeans, tribes from the desert to the south.

In 625 BC Nabopolassar seized the throne of Babylon and began a vigorous campaign of conquest. Assyria was attacked and Nineveh, the capital, was destroyed in 612 BC. Seven years later, Nebuchadnezzar became king of Babylonia. He spent vast amounts of money restoring old religious temples and building canals. He is probably most famous for another great work of construction - the Hanging Gardens of Babylon, a huge roof-garden supported on brick arches.

The rebirth of the Babylonian empire did not last long, however. Nebuchadnezzar's successor, Nabonidus, angered the powerful priests of Marduk and abandoned the throne to his son. Eventually, Babylon fell to the newly emerging Persian empire in 539 BC.

Below: This boundary stone warned people that they were about to enter Babylonian territory.

THE HITTITES

In the period from about 2000 to 1200 BC, the Levant, the area around the eastern coastline of the Mediterranean Sea from the Nile in Egypt to southeast Anatolia (in what is now Turkey), was occupied by a number of independent city-states. Because they had all grown very wealthy by trading in gold, copper, and pottery, they became targets for invasion by the kingdoms in the surrounding regions, including the Egyptians, the Mitannians of northern Mesopotamia, and the Hittites of Anatolia. The Hittites had developed from a group of cities into a unified state in about 1650 BC, and by the fourteenth century BC they had replaced the Mitannians as Egypt's main rivals for the Levant.

Warfare and Diplomacy

During their almost constant battles for control of the Levant, the three empires developed new ways of fighting. In around 1800 BC fast, two-wheeled war chariots appeared. They were very strongly built yet light enough to be lifted by one man. Each chariot was pulled by a team of horses and manned by archers in bronze armour, who shot bronze-tipped arrows at their enemies. Many of the cities in the region had strong defensive walls, and so sieges became common. Weapons such as battering rams and siege towers were invented to break down the cities' defences. In turn, the defenders devised protective ramparts with steep slopes in front of the city walls to stop attackers using their new weapons. However, even that could not prevent some cities from being overrun and destroyed.

At the same time as the wars were being fought, the various empires attempted to make peace. Clay tablets have been found, written by both the Hittites, in a language called Akkadian, and the Egyptians, in which one side or the other suggested bringing the fighting to an end.

Bogazköy

The capital of the Hittite empire was at Bogazköy, in central Anatolia. Although the surrounding area is very dry, the site for the city was chosen because water was available from a river that flowed around it. What is more, the rocky terrain formed a natural defensive barrier against attack. Bogazköy was one of the group of cities that were united as a single Hittite state in 1650 BC. As the Hittites increased their power, they rebuilt and extended their capital. The remains of the city walls, which show how the city grew, can still be seen today. They were extremely strong, and in some places were built on top of high ramparts faced in stone. The gates that led into the city were decorated with carved lions and Hittite gods.

When archaeologists excavated the citadel at Bogazköy in 1908, they found the ruins of a royal palace, which had a massive hall 32 m square, five huge temples, and two archives containing 3,000 cuneiform clay tablets. These tablets, with literary, legal, and religious texts, gave the first clue to the size and sophistication of the empire created by the Hittites. It seems that this empire, which was previously almost unknown, may have included all the lands from the Aegean Sea in the west to the Euphrates valley in the east.

The Sea Peoples

In the twelfth century BC, all of the major states in the Levant came under attack from unknown raiders from the sea, and one by one their empires collapsed. The Hittite empire fell in around 1200 BC, and although the Egyptians remained, their power was seriously weakened.

Below: The Lion Gate at the Hittite capital, Bogazköy.

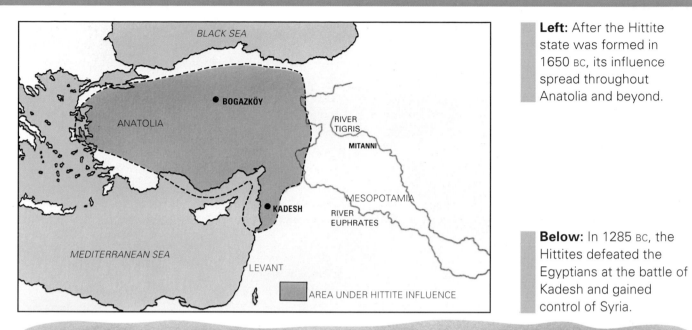

Left: After the Hittite state was formed in 1650 BC, its influence spread throughout Anatolia and beyond.

Below: In 1285 BC, the Hittites defeated the Egyptians at the battle of Kadesh and gained control of Syria.

HITTITE CITIES UNITED 1650 BC • HITTITES DEFEATED BY SEA PEOPLES c.1200 BC

MYCENAEAN GREECE

In the middle of the sixteenth century BC, a new power emerged in the eastern Mediterranean - the state of Mycenae. It was centred on the city of Mycenae, on the Peloponnese peninsula at the southern tip of mainland Greece. Greece is a mountainous country, and a number of other states grew up on

Left: An ivory carving of a Mycenaean warrior's head. Soldier's helmets were made from the tusks of wild boar.

Below left: A terracotta figure representing a Mycenaean mother-goddess. It was made about 3,300 years ago.

Below Right: Mycenae was protected by a high stone wall. But around 1200 BC it was attacked and destroyed.

RISE OF MYCENAEANS c.1550 BC • STRONGLY INFLUENCED BY MINOAN CIVILIZATION

the fertile plains between the highlands. None of these, however, could challenge the Mycenaeans.

In some ways the Mycenaean civilization was rather like that of the Minoans. The Mycenaeans' language, a form of Greek known as Linear B, has also been found in Crete, evidence of the fact that there was close contact between the two communities. The Mycenaeans decorated their palaces with colourful frescoes and imitated Minoan pottery designs. In other ways, however, the two civilizations were quite different. While Minoan Crete had been fairly peace-loving, preferring trade to conquest, the Mycenaeans were much more warlike. Their strong navy enabled them to control a large area of the eastern Mediterranean, while the army overpowered several neighbouring Greek regions, including Attica and Boeotia, and captured Crete. They also attacked the heavily fortified citadel of Troy, on the Aegean coast of Anatolia, but without success.

Warlike Times

There is much evidence for the fact that warfare was an important part of life in Greece at this time. The city of Mycenae itself was heavily fortified, with a high stone wall up to 7 m thick. Other Greek citadels were also reinforced with strong defences during the Mycenaean period, which suggests that they were increasingly fearful of attack. Painted pottery and frescoes show soldiers with long spears, shields, and helmets made from the tusks of wild boar. Mycenaean warriors' tombs have been found containing vast quantities of swords and daggers, their blades often beautifully decorated with scenes of battle. The armies of Mycenae used war chariots, similar to those used by other civilizations, but Greece's rugged terrain made it difficult to move chariots and men quickly. Their solution to this problem was to build a network of roads throughout the Peloponnese and in the states they conquered.

Prosperity and Decline

Mycenae became a wealthy state quite quickly; one of its earliest rulers was buried in about 1550 BC with 5 kg of gold. Not all of the Mycenaeans' prosperity came from plundering other states; they also established a trading network throughout the Mediterranean. Copper and tin were imported (to make bronze), as were gold, ivory, and gemstones. Exports of pottery, bronze weapons, jewellery, olive oil, wine, and wool reached Syria, Egypt, southern Italy, and even as far as Britain.

During the thirteenth century BC Mycenaean power gradually began to wane, but when the end came it was swift. Invaders, possibly the Dorians of northern Greece, stormed into Mycenae's territories and destroyed its palaces. The great citadel of Mycenae itself went up in flames a short time after 1200 BC. The invaders had no interest in civilization; writing disappeared from Greece and did not return for several centuries.

MYCENAE CONQUERS SOUTHERN GREECE • CIVILIZATION DESTROYED c.1200 BC

THE PHOENICIANS

The country of Phoenicia was at the eastern end of the Mediterranean, in the area known as the Levant. It occupied a narrow coastal plain some 320 km long and 30 km wide, between the sea and the mountains of Lebanon. Phoenicia consisted of a number of city-states dotted along the coast, including Tyre, Sidon, Berytus, Byblos, and Aradus. It was from these ports that the Phoenicians established a trading empire that was to cover most of the Mediterranean.

Craft and Trade

The craftsmen of Phoenicia were not particularly inventive; they took their artistic ideas from earlier civilizations, especially Egypt, and used them to produce work in bronze, ivory, wood, and textiles. When their products became popular, the craftsmen mass-produced them, turning out hundreds of the same item, all with the same pattern. Phoenician ships travelled to countries further and further afield, exchanging these products for other goods that were needed at home, such as silver, wheat, and slaves. In order to protect and increase their trade, the Phoenicians established outposts in other parts of the Mediterranean, including Carthage and Tingis in North Africa, Malaca in southern Spain, and Nora on the island of Sardinia.

But they were not to have things all their own way. From about 800 BC Greek city-states began to trade throughout the Aegean, the Black Sea, and much of the Mediterranean. They followed similar routes to those of the Mycenaeans before them, but were a much more powerful force to contend with. Like the Phoenicians, the Greeks set up colonies of their own - in southern Russia, Italy, eastern Spain, and elsewhere. Wherever possible, the ships of these trading empires avoided each other; the Greeks operated in the northern Mediterranean while the Phoenicians concentrated their efforts in the south and west. Nonetheless, when their paths did cross, the two sides almost certainly fought. Phoenician warships were the most advanced of their time: they could be propelled either by wind in the sail or by oarsmen, and had a ram for piercing enemy ships.

Spreading the Word

During their trading expeditions overseas, the Phoenicians spread their culture among the peoples they came into contact with. They carried with them one particularly important gift - an alphabet.

The script which the Phoenicians developed, like many other things in their civilization, came originally from earlier times and had its roots in Egypt. Over the centuries the Egyptians' hieroglyphics had been adapted by other groups, and the Phoenicians continued this process. They created an alphabet that used only 22 signs, each of which represented a sound. This made it easy to learn and meant that specially trained scribes were no longer needed.

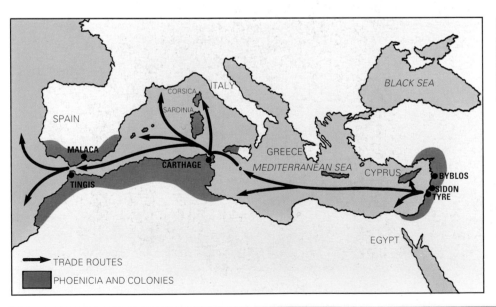

Left: From its heartland at the eastern end of the Mediterranean, Phoenicia established a large trading empire.

Right: The Phoenicians built fast warships to protect their trading ships from Greek attacks.

COLONIES IN MEDITERRANEAN 1200-800 BC • SIMPLE ALPHABET DEVELOPED

Phoenicia's trading empire was at its height between 1200 and 800 BC. In about 700 BC their main city-state, Tyre, was captured by the Assyrians and later came under the control of the Persian empire. The colony at Carthage became the centre from which the southern and western Mediterranean was controlled, and it developed into an independent power that challenged first the Greeks and then the mighty Roman empire (see pages 52-53).

Below: The Phoenicians spread their language and alphabet throughout their Mediterranean trading empire.

THE HEBREWS

In the second century BC there were many nomadic groups in the deserts of the Middle East, and the Hebrews were one of these. According to the Old Testament of the Bible, their story began with a tribal leader called Abraham, who left his home in the Sumerian city of Ur some time after 2000 BC and began a long journey to the country of Canaan (now called Palestine). His descendants settled there in about 1400 BC, but following a great famine, many moved on to Egypt.

The Hebrews stayed in Egypt for several centuries. At first they lived in freedom, but were later enslaved and cruelly treated. Finally, in about 1200 BC, they were taken out of captivity by a new leader, Moses. After Moses' death, the Hebrews crossed the River Jordan and returned to Canaan. There, they captured the city of Jericho, and then conquered the whole country.

According to the Bible, the Hebrews were guided throughout their journeys by God, whom they called Yahweh. During the time of Moses, their belief in a single, powerful god became more clearly defined. Traditionally, the Ten Commandments were revealed to Moses on Mount Sinai and these laws formed the basis of the "covenant", or agreement, between Yahweh and the Hebrews. Many other laws about both everyday life and worship were also written down at about this time.

The Hebrew Kings

The Hebrews were divided into 12 separate tribes. For many years, they came under attack from enemies on the borders of Canaan, especially the Philistines. They eventually decided to elect a king to lead them against their attackers. They chose Saul, who became their ruler in about 1020 BC. When Saul was defeated in battle 20 years later, David was made king. He set up his capital at Jerusalem, in an area that did not belong to any of the 12 tribes. However, there were already disagreements between the tribes in the north of the country and those in the south, and these were to emerge again later.

David's son, Solomon, brought some prosperity to the country when he was king, mainly by increasing trade. He is also known for the buildings he constructed - cities, fortifications, and an elaborate temple at Jerusalem. After Solomon's death in about 922 BC, the conflict between the northern and southern tribes came to a head, and the country was divided in two: the kingdom of Judah in the south and the kingdom of Israel in the north.

Below: The Ark of the Covenant - the symbol of God's presence - is carried into Jerusalem.

Far right: Jews inside the Masada fortress held out against Roman attacks during AD 72 and 73.

Right: Baal was regarded by Hebrews as a "false god"; they worshipped Yahweh.

The Fall of Judah

From about 600 BC, the Hebrew lands were invaded by empires beyond their borders. Israel was conquered by the Assyrians in 721 BC, and Judah was dominated first by Egypt and then by the Babylonians, who destroyed Jerusalem in 587 BC. Many Hebrews were taken as captives to Babylon. When the Persians defeated the Babylonians in 539 BC, they gave permission for the Hebrews, or Israelites, to return to their land. The returning exiles came to be known as Jews.

After Persian rule, the Israelites became part of Alexander the Great's empire (see pages 56-57), and were later governed by Egypt and then the Seleucids. Finally, in 164 BC, Jerusalem was retaken by the Jews, only to be captured once more in 63 BC by the Romans. From 34 BC the land was ruled on behalf of the Romans by King Herod. It was during Herod's reign that Jesus Christ was born.

During the first two centuries AD, the Jewish people rebelled several times against the Romans. In AD 70 the Romans destroyed the temple in Jerusalem, and many Jews fled to other countries. In AD 135 the Roman emperor established the colony of Aelia Capitoliana on the site of ruined Jerusalem. Only non-Jews were allowed to live there.

THE CELTS

Celtic people may have lived in Europe for several thousand years before the birth of Christ, but it was not until about 800 BC that they developed a culture of their own. Most of what we now know about them comes from the graves in which they were buried, the remains of their fortresses, and their art.

Iron Age Europe

The technique of making tools and weapons from iron played an important part in Celtic culture. It was first discovered in western Asia between 2000 and 1500 BC, but soon spread in all directions, reaching central Europe in around 1000 BC and Britain 300 years later. At first iron goods were quite rare and expensive. However, the ore from which iron is made is plentiful in Europe and slowly the new metal replaced bronze. Iron swords and other weapons came first, followed by tools and other everyday objects. The metal was heated until it became soft, beaten into the shape that was required, and then allowed to cool.

Because iron is harder than bronze, its discovery changed the way in which war was fought. Tougher, sharper weapons were more effective than bronze ones and, as iron-working spread, more people could be equipped with them. Iron could also be used to strengthen defences. For example, it is believed that the timber ramparts of one Celtic settlement, Manching in Bavaria, were held in position using 300 tonnes of iron nails. The use of iron even affected the

Below: Many Celts lived in farms and villages grouped around a hillfort or fortified town.

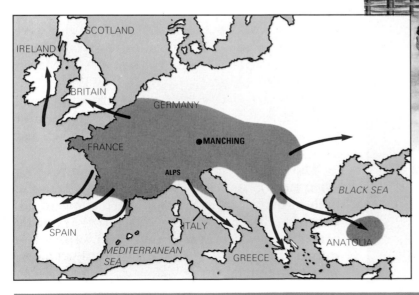

Left: From southern Germany and the Alps, the Celts spread throughout much of Europe.

FIRST USE OF IRON IN EUROPE c.1000 BC • RISE OF CELTIC CULTURE c.800 BC

Above: Maiden Castle. Celts in Britain built huge hillforts like this one to protect themselves from attack.

landscape of Europe: with sharp iron tools, large areas of forest could be cut down to make room for settlements and increase agricultural land.

The Spread of Celtic Culture

The early heartland of the Celts was in southern Germany and the eastern Alps. From about 800 BC they began to expand their territory. By 500 BC Celtic-speaking people had settled in France and Spain; by 400 BC they had moved into parts of Italy and attacked Rome in 390; and by 275 BC they had reached Greece and Anatolia. At some time after 450 BC the Celts reached Britain, although the exact date is not known.

During the same period in which they were spreading outwards, other important changes were taking place among the Celts. They came into contact with the peoples of the Mediterranean - especially in the overseas colonies set up by the Greeks - and this led to a rapid increase in trade. From this time, Celtic nobles were buried with fine, valuable objects imported from other countries.

The Celts themselves were excellent craftsmen. The graves of chieftains, princesses, and other rich people contained beautiful bronze vessels used for pouring and drinking wine, gold neck-rings, and decorated sword sheaths.

In about 300 BC the Celts began to use coins, which were similar in design to the Greek money of the time. Around 150 years later, large fortified sites, called *oppida*, started to appear. They were rather like small towns, with timber houses, barns, storehouses, and workshops where bronze and iron goods, pottery, textiles, and coins were made.

The Celts continued to trade with the Mediterranean, although their earlier Greek trading partners had by this time been replaced by the Romans. Within a short time, the Celts were to suffer Roman influence of a different kind. As Rome grew, not even the heavily fortified hilltop sites could protect the Celts. By 100 BC southern France had become a Roman colony, and within 250 years most of the remaining Celtic territory had been captured. Only Ireland and northern Scotland stayed beyond the Romans' grasp, and Celtic culture survived there until the Middle Ages.

TRADE WITH GREEK COLONIES FROM 600 BC • CELTS FALL TO ROMANS BY AD 150

THE ETRUSCANS

In about 800 BC a remarkable civilization began in Italy, in the fertile area between the River Tiber, the River Po, and the Apennine Mountains. Much of this region is still known as Tuscany, after the Etruscan people who lived there.

No one knows for sure where the Etruscans came from. They may have been local people who developed their culture through contact with Greek traders, or they could have come from western Asia after the collapse of the Hittite and Mycenaean empires. Whatever their origins, they were to have an important effect on the history of Italy.

Cities, Trade, and Culture

The first signs of Etruscan civilization were two groups of prosperous cities that grew up, one in the

Below: A Greek vase found at the city of Vulci. Many vases and other works of art were imported by the Etruscans.

north and the other to the south. Both groups depended on agriculture, although the southern cities seem also to have had strong trading links with other lands, especially Greece.

Vases and other works of art were imported, while bronze and black pottery (known as *bucchero*) were exported. The Etruscans were highly skilled in the creation of bronze pots, brooches, mirrors, and candelabra, and the statues that they made from terracotta were also extremely popular.

Greeks had settled in southern Italy much earlier, and the Etruscans took advantage of this to extend their trade southwards. However, traders transporting goods along this route frequently came under attack from hill tribes. The Etruscans' overseas trade was also badly hit in 474 BC when they were defeated by the Carthaginians in a sea battle at Cumae, near what is now Naples.

Apart from their own achievements, the Etruscans are important because of the part they played in the growth of Roman civilization. Their engineering skills - they built impressive road networks, canals, and underground tunnels to carry rivers *under* roads - had a direct influence on early Rome. Their religion, with its complex group of human-like gods, was also echoed later by Roman ideas.

We know very little about how Etruscan cities were run. This is mainly because no one has yet been able to understand the Etruscan language fully. Although the characters used were very similar to those of the Greek alphabet, the language itself is unlike any other known today. Scholars have been able to translate some simple texts found on tomb paintings, but the few long texts which still exist are not really understood.

The End of the Etruscans

The decline of the Etruscan civilization, from around 300 BC, was caused partly by the fact that their cities were never truly united. The main reason, however, was the rapid growth of the civilization to the south of their lands - Rome.

As it increased in power, Rome was able to control the Etruscans' trade routes. The Romans also conquered the city of Veii and forced Caere to become their ally, after which the remaining Etruscan cities fell one by one under the power of Rome. This process happened quite gradually; there was no all-out war, although there were occasional battles. The Etruscans came to realize that their future was tied to that of Rome, and they attempted to make the best of their situation. By about 100 BC all the main Etruscan cities were part of the Roman Republic. They had played an important part in the development of Roman civilization, and in the end that great and powerful civilization took them over.

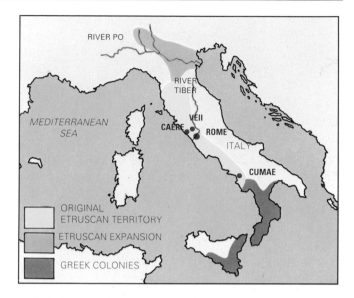

Below: Many Etruscan tombs were built like underground houses where the dead could live in the afterlife.

Right: The Etruscan civilization developed around Cumae in southern Italy and Veii and Caere in the north.

THE ASSYRIANS

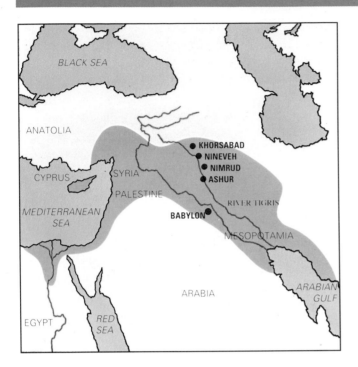

Following the collapse of the Hittite empire and the decline of the Egyptians around 1200 BC, the city-states which were scattered throughout Mesopotamia and the Levant were once again independent. They were not to remain so for very long, however.

The Rise of Assyria

The state of Assyria first emerged in about 2360 BC, and was grouped around the heavily fortified city of Ashur, on the River Tigris. In time, the Assyrians captured lands to the west and extended their rule as far as the coast of the Mediterranean. However, they were not able to hold their possessions for long and their territory shrank back to a small area around Ashur. By 911 BC Assyrian kings were once again leading their armies on raids to capture more land. Their conquests began under King Adadnirari II and his grandson Ashurnasirpal II, and the Assyrian empire reached its height under Sargon II in the late eighth century BC. At that time it included the

Above: The Assyrian empire as it was at its height under Sargon II.

Below: Assyrian kings enjoyed hunting, especially lions and other dangerous wild animals.

BIRTH OF ASSYRIAN STATE c.2360 BC • EMPIRE REACHES ITS PEAK c.721-705 BC

Assyrian heartland around Ashur, the Levantine city-states, Syria, Palestine, Cyprus, and, to the west, parts of Anatolia.

In 880 BC the Assyrian capital had been moved from Ashur to Nimrud and by the time Sargon became king (721 BC) it had moved again, to Khorsabad. From the stone carvings, called reliefs, which decorated the royal palaces in the capitals, we can see how the Assyrians were able to conquer so much territory. They were remarkably inventive in warfare: the palace reliefs show several different types of infantry, armoured cavalry, horse-drawn chariots with shield-bearers and archers, and soldiers besieging cities by digging tunnels and using battering rams and ladders.

In order to hold on to their possessions, the Assyrians divided their empire into provinces, each ruled by a governor and occupied by soldiers. Conquered states and cities were forced to pay the Assyrians money to prevent further attack, and this was one source of the empire's great wealth. The coastal cities of the Levant provided more in the form of harbour taxes on cargoes, and were also used to import luxury goods. The Taurus mountains in Anatolia were rich in iron, lead, and copper, while the fertile crop-growing lands of Mesopotamia fed the towns and cities of Assyria and its armies.

The Rise and Fall of Nineveh

Around the end of Sargon's reign (705 BC) the capital moved again, this time to Nineveh. The city became the greatest of all the Assyrian capitals, dominated by a huge citadel containing palaces and temples. The royal palace had a network of throne-rooms and reception halls where court officials, foreign ambassadors, and conquered leaders could be received. Nearby was the royal arsenal where both military equipment and goods plundered during conquest were stored.

As well as being the most impressive Assyrian capital, Nineveh was also the last. Not surprisingly, the empire had many enemies. Chief among these were the Babylonians to the south, under their new king Nabopolassar, the Scythians to the north, and the Medes to the east. At the end of the seventh century BC these forces joined to overthrow the

Assyrian empire. Nineveh and Nimrud were destroyed in 612 BC and the power of the Assyrians fell with them. The structure of their empire lived on, however, and was taken over by the Babylonians.

Below: A winged, human-headed bull, which guarded the entrance to Khorsabad.

ARCHAIC GREECE

Several centuries after the power of the Mycenaeans declined in about 1100 BC, a number of small city-states grew up in the fertile plains between the mountains of Greece, on the islands of the Aegcan Sea, and in the lands that bordered the sea. Each city-state had its own king, government, and laws, and often its own army, too. Around the central city, or *polis*, were the farms and villages of the ordinary people, who lived by growing corn, vegetables, and olives, and rearing goats for milk and cheese.

The Greek World

The Greek city-states were all independent, and were only linked by the fact that their citizens all spoke Greek and worshipped Greek gods. One innovation that increased their links was the Olympic Games, which were first held in 776 BC, and in which people from all over the Greek world participated. Another was money in the form of coins, which was invented in about 600 BC. The first coins were made of electrum - a mixture of gold and silver - but later they were solid silver. Although most people still bartered, that is exchanged one type of goods for another, coins came to be used by traders for buying and selling. Some of the first silver coins were made in Athens; on one side they had a picture of an owl, the symbol of Athena, the goddess of the city.

From about 750 BC, ships from the Greek city-states began to sail to other regions. They carried people who were searching for land of their own, or who were simply hoping to trade. Cities such as Corinth, Eretria, and Megara set up colonies in southern Italy, Spain, North Africa, around the Black Sea, and in south-west Anatolia. Some of these colonies are still important cities today - Naples in Italy, and Marseille in France, for example. In this way, Greek culture was spread throughout the Mediterranean region.

Athens, Sparta, and Persia

By the fifth century BC two states - Athens and Sparta - had become extremely powerful. At first they stood together in order to fight off the armies of Persia. In 490 BC the huge Persian empire launched an attack on Athens. Their ships put ashore an army of 20,000 men, but in the battle of Marathon which followed, the Greeks triumphed. Ten years later, a much larger Persian army was ready to attack again. It was so large that it could not be transported across the Aegean by ship. Instead the soldiers marched overland towards Greece, keeping close to the shore so that food and other supplies could be carried to them

Below: A Greek infantryman from between 600 and 500 BC.

by sea. The Greeks realized that if the Persian navy were destroyed, the army would be weakened. While the advance of the Persian army was being delayed by the Spartans, the Persians' ships were lured to the island of Salamis, where in 480 BC most of them were sunk or scattered by the Athenian navy. The Persian king Xerxes could only watch helplessly as his fleet was destroyed.

Despite their co-operation against the Persians, by 431 BC Sparta and Athens were fighting one another in the Peloponnesian War, which was to last 27 years. The war was a disaster for Athens. After years of stalemate, the balance tilted in Sparta's favour when the great Persian empire began supplying it with money to build new ships. The Spartan commander, Lysander, defeated the Athenian navy and then besieged Athens itself. Unable to obtain food, the Athenians starved through the winter of 405 BC and surrendered the following spring.

Above: Some of the main Greek city-states. Each had its own king and government.

Below: Wrestling was a popular sport in Greece. It helped soldiers keep fit and strong for battle.

AFRICAN CIVILIZATIONS

About 10,000 years ago, the area that is now the Sahara Desert was not desert at all, but wet grassland on which farmers herded cattle and grew wheat and barley. After about 2500 BC, the climate changed and the grasslands started to dry out. As a result, the farmers moved south into tropical Africa to find new crop-growing areas. There they began cultivating millet, sorghum (a type of cereal grass), and yams; in places where the land was covered with dense forest, the people lived principally by fishing instead of farming.

The first civilization to develop in sub-Saharan Africa, that is Africa south of the Sahara and Egypt, was the kingdom of Kush on the banks of the River Nile, in what is now Ethiopia. From about 600 BC its capital, Meroë, was an important centre for iron-working. Kush was eventually invaded and conquered by an army from Axum (see pages 46-47) in about AD 350.

Africa in the Iron Age

One of the most important events in the development of the rest of sub-Saharan Africa was the manufacture of iron, which began there in around 600 BC. In most other civilizations, copper and bronze had been made before iron-working was discovered, but in Africa people seem to have gone straight from using stone tools to making iron ones. Iron-working technology was probably brought from the Phoenician colonies on the North African coast, rather than from Kush, and carried across the Sahara along trade routes from the Mediterranean.

Among the first Africans to manufacture iron were the Nok people, who had lived in what is now the West African state of Nigeria since about 900 BC. Among the few remains of Nok culture are a number of terracotta heads, some of which are life-sized and were clearly modelled on real people. They were probably used for religious rituals.

The Spread of Agriculture

People living in West Africa - including, perhaps, those of the Nok culture - began to move into other parts of Africa from around 500 BC. As they did so, they spread their language, Bantu, and their iron-working skills. Some moved south through what is now Zaïre to Namibia, while others settled around Lake Victoria in the east. The manufacture of iron was quickly taken up by the farming communities who already lived in these areas.

Bantu-speakers continued to spread south in the first few centuries AD and they introduced iron-working to southern Africa. They also took with them knowledge of another important technique - farming. The inhabitants of southern Africa, including the San and Khoi-khoi peoples, were hunter gatherers. The Bantu-speakers steadily laid claim to the most fertile lands they found and either pushed out or absorbed the native populations. Eventually, farmers using iron tools spread throughout southern Africa, except for the far south-west, which was too dry for crop-growing.

By about AD 1000, most of the peoples of sub-Saharan Africa lived in settled farming communities,

Left: This rock painting was done by people living in the Saharan Desert around 8,000 years ago.

KINGDOM OF KUSH EMERGES c.900 BC • IRON-WORKING IN WEST AFRICA c.600 BC

and the first powerful states, such as Ghana in the west, and Zimbabwe in the east, had begun to emerge. These new states depended on trade: gold, ivory, and slaves were exported in return for glass, porcelain, silk, beads, and shells. The main trading partners, especially in East Africa, were Arab merchants, some of whom settled along the coast.

From the fifteenth century, however, a new influence appeared in Africa - Europeans. Coming from Portugal, Britain, Holland, France, Belgium, and other countries in Europe, they first established trading networks and then claimed possession of the entire continent. By 1913 there was hardly an area of Africa that was not part of a European empire.

Below: A dwelling hut made from grass laid over a wooden frame.

Right: The spread of Bantu-speaking peoples and iron working in Africa.

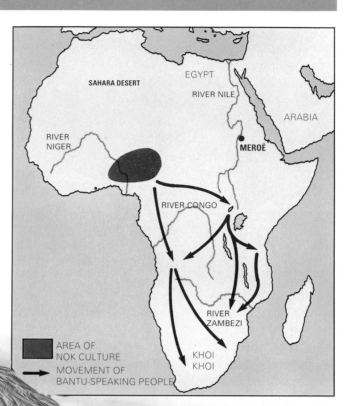

BANTU-SPEAKERS SPREAD FARMING AND USE OF IRON SOUTHWARDS FROM 500 BC

THE CARTHAGINIANS

The city of Carthage, on the coast of what is now Tunisia, was founded in about 814 BC by the Phoenicians (see pages 32-33). Its purpose was to protect the Phoenicians' trade routes between their own cities on the eastern Mediterranean coast and Spain. During the sixth century BC the Phoenician cities were captured first by the Babylonians and then the Persians, and Phoenician settlements on Sicily came under attack from the Greeks. Carthage went to the aid of the Sicilian settlements, and further increased its power by joining the Etruscans to defeat the Greeks in a sea battle in 535 BC.

The Carthaginian Empire

By the end of the sixth century BC, Carthage was an independent state, and was tied to the original Phoenician cities only by having the same religion. In the century that followed, the Carthaginians created an empire of their own and became the most powerful force in the western Mediterranean.

The empire was created to defend the Carthaginians' trade, and it was trade that brought the empire its prosperity. The major sources of wealth were silver and tin from Spain, and gold from Africa. Carthage also traded with the Greeks in the Aegean and in Sicily, probably selling them food. Goods manufactured in Carthage were doubtless sold abroad, although the city's craftsmen were not especially original or skilful.

In the early days of the empire, Carthage's main rivals were the Greeks, who attempted to capture its settlements and trade routes. The Carthaginians quickly raised large armies of mercenaries - paid foreign soldiers - to fight off the Greek threat.

Carthage and Rome

The most serious threat, however, was to come from Rome. After the Carthaginians had dominated the western Mediterranean for 300 years, they came face to face with the might of the Roman Republic. The two powers had signed treaties in 508 and 348 BC, recognizing each other's authority over certain territories and trade routes. But as Rome expanded further and further, peace could not last. Of the three Punic Wars between Rome and Carthage, the first was fought mainly on and around Sicily from 264 to 241 BC. When peace terms were signed, Carthage gave up Sicily and Sardinia.

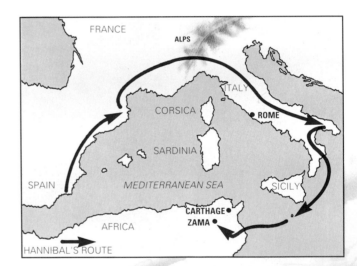

Above right: The route of Hannibal's great journey during the Second Punic War (218-201 BC).

Right: Hannibal led his army across the Alps in 218 BC and then beat the Romans several times in battle.

The Second Punic War (218-201 BC) began rather better for the Carthaginians, when Hannibal, one of their generals, marched an army from Spain, through the Alps, and almost to the gates of Rome. His army used elephants in battle and partly thanks to these four-legged "tanks", he was able to score some dramatic victories. However, he was fighting a long way from home and could not always get the supplies and reinforcements he needed.

A great commander, Hannibal managed to control his army in enemy territory for 15 years before being beaten by the sheer size of the Roman army. Rome took over most of Spain in 206 BC and Hannibal returned to Africa in 203 BC - that was one of the terms of the peace treaty. A Roman general,

Scipio, inflicted the final defeat upon Hannibal at the battle of Zama in 202 BC. Carthage was forced to surrender its fleet and all of its overseas territories.

On his return to Africa, Hannibal became the leader of Carthage and attempted to make it a more unified state. This aroused the suspicion of the Romans, who forced him into exile and constantly pursued him. He committed suicide in 183 rather than allow himself to be captured.

Rome also became alarmed when Carthage once again began to build up its trade. In the Third Punic War, which began in 149 BC, the Romans were determined to put an end to Carthage. Three years later they succeeded: the city was captured and completely destroyed in 146 BC.

Right: This is all that remains of the city of Carthage.

CLASSICAL GREECE

In the fifth century BC, Athens became the most important city-state in Greece and the entire Mediterranean. Despite its defeat at the hands of the Spartans (see pages 44-45), it held on to its position of prestige for more than 400 years. Throughout this time, known as the Classical period, Athens was the cultural and intellectual centre of the known world.

Classical Civilization

Among the greatest achievements of Classical Greece were the many advances that were made in sculpture and architecture. These two art forms were joined together in one stunning creation - the Parthenon temple. When the Persian army attacked Athens in 480 BC, they destroyed the Temple of Athena which stood on the Acropolis, the steep hill in the centre of the city. The Parthenon was built in 462 BC to replace that temple. It was constructed entirely from local marble - even including the roof tiles - and was one of the largest temples in Greece. A carved frieze ran around the top of the main building facing the external columns. This showed scenes from the life of the goddess Athena, and from the procession that took place in her honour, the Panathenaia.

Some years later, the Theatre of Dionysus was built below the Acropolis. It was here that the works of the great Athenian playwrights, such as Sophocles and Aristophanes, were performed. Their plays - tragedies, comedies, and histories - often centred around the events and heroes of Greek myths.

In the Classical period, science began to develop. Great strides were made in medicine and in mathematics. Greek philosophers, such as Socrates, Plato, and Aristotle, wrote about the Universe and the place of humans within it; for the first time people were regarded as individuals with their own destinies.

Religion

The Greeks worshipped many gods and goddesses and had hundreds of legends about their lives and deeds. There were local gods and other, more important, ones who looked after every aspect of life and death. According to legend, the first gods were created by Mother Earth and were known as Titans. In Classical times, the most important gods, including Zeus, who ruled over all the others, were thought to live on Mount Olympus in north-east Greece.

Above: Pericles was the most important statesman of Classical Greece.

Below: The Panathenaia procession was held to honour the goddess Athena.

PARTHENON TEMPLE BUILT 462 BC • BEGINNINGS OF DEMOCRACY IN ATHENS

The Birth of Democracy

The homes of the ordinary Athenians were nothing like the splendid public buildings that were constructed in Classical times. Most people lived in small houses with bare earth floors, grouped around courtyards. The streets were narrow and unpaved, and there was no adequate sewage system.

However, the citizens of Athens benefited in another way from the age in which they lived. Unlike other city-states, Athens gave its people a right to influence how they were governed. The city was ruled by an assembly which was elected by the people, and citizens were allowed to speak to the assembly about any matter they chose. Public figures who were thought to be too powerful or were not doing their job properly could be expelled by the voters. This was not true democracy, as only male citizens over 18 years old had political rights - women, slaves, and non-Athenians were not allowed to vote. But it was the first step towards the system of government we know today.

One man, Pericles, became effectively the head of the Athenian government. The people trusted his advice and re-elected him every year from about 443 until his death in 429 BC.

RISE OF CLASSICAL DRAMA, ART, PHILOSOPHY, AND SCIENCE

THE MACEDONIANS

The land of Macedonia, to the north of Greece, was a tribal kingdom until the beginning of the fourth century BC. It was not very unified and, because of that, was frequently attacked by its neighbours.

The Rule of Philip

The man who did most to build up the power of Macedonia was Philip, who came to power in 359 BC, when he was made regent to govern on behalf of a new king who was too young to rule. Philip quickly took the throne himself and, after first strengthening his army, defeated the neighbouring kingdoms, creating a stronghold from which he could conquer lands further afield. By 339 BC the Macedonian empire stretched from the River Danube in the north to the Aegean Sea in the south, and from the Adriatic coast in the west to the Black Sea in the east.

Unlike many previous conquerors, Philip did not destroy the cities and lands he invaded. He subdued their kings and royal families, but allowed the captured cities and tribes to govern themselves. He built new towns, improved agriculture, and increased the amount of money the lands could provide. Men from all parts of the empire were enlisted into his army and, thanks to his clever administration, Philip was able to pay them without demanding high taxes from his subjects.

Philip pursued a different policy with the Greek states from that which had brought him the rest of his empire. He tried diplomacy instead of conquest, and managed to win over most of Greece to his idea of a league of self-governing Greek states. Only Athens, Thebes, and a few others opposed him openly. When the two sides met in battle at Chaeronae in 338 BC, the Macedonians were triumphant. As a result, all the Greek states apart from Sparta agreed to join forces with Macedonia against the great power of the Persian empire.

Philip's successes brought great power and prosperity to the Macedonians, and he was admired by many of his people. However, like all rulers, Philip had enemies and in 336 BC he was assassinated. This blow might have brought about the end of the Macedonian empire if it had not been for the extraordinary abilities of the man who succeeded Philip - his son Alexander.

Alexander the Great

By acting quickly and intelligently, Alexander held the empire together. With a mixture of diplomacy and armed force he put down rebellions in Greece, and in 334 BC he turned his attention to the Persians. Crossing from Europe to Asia, he defeated them in three great battles, the last at Gaugamela in 331 BC, and overthrew their empire. He then began recruiting Asians into his army, building it up to 170,000 men, and leading it further east, as far as India.

Alexander next planned to conquer Arabia and return to the Mediterranean. With this in mind, he trained some of his new Asian recruits to oversee

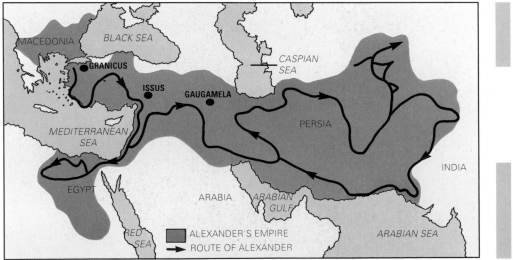

Left: The empire of Alexander the Great at the time of his death in 323 BC.

Right: At its largest, Alexander's army contained 170,000 soldiers, many of whom came from conquered lands.

PHILIP OF MACEDON RULES 359-336 BC • ALEXANDER CONQUERS PERSIANS 331 BC

Above: Part of a mosaic showing Alexander the Great in battle.

their own lands. But, at the height of his power, the greatest conqueror in history died of a fever. He was just 32 years old. In his short reign he had created a multi-racial kingdom, in which people of all nationalities could succeed if they were talented enough. Perhaps his most memorable achievement in Asia was the creation of 70 new towns - often called Alexandria - with mixed populations of Macedonians, Greeks, and Asians.

After Alexander's death, the empire was split into a number of kingdoms ruled by kings who had been generals in the army. These new kings fought among themselves for control of the heart of the empire - Macedonia itself. Their squabbles went on without interruption until 279 BC, when the Gauls of western Europe invaded. They were turned back and Macedonia continued, with occasional gains and losses of territory, for several decades. Then, in 200 BC, it came up against the growing power of Rome. Years of sporadic warfare followed until the Romans seized all Macedonian lands in 148 BC.

DEATH OF ALEXANDER THE GREAT 323 BC • ROMANS CAPTURE MACEDONIA 148 BC

THE ROMAN REPUBLIC

The first settlement at Rome was a small group of huts built on the Palatine hill during the ninth century BC. In the seventh century, when central Italy was ruled by the Etruscans, Rome developed from a small village to an important city. As the Etruscans' power declined, that of Rome grew, and in around 510 BC the Roman people drove the Etruscans out of their city and established a republic.

Below: A scene in the Senate, Rome's governing body.

Right: Rome and its surroundings at the time of the republic.

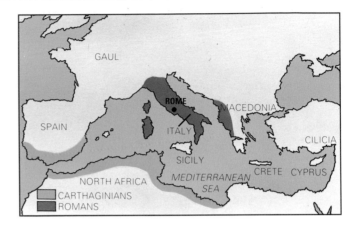

BIRTH OF ROMAN REPUBLIC 510 BC • WAR WITH CARTHAGE 264-241 AND 218-201 BC

ROMAN GODS

Here are just a few of the Romans' many gods and goddesses. At the top are Juno, the goddess of women, and her husband Jupiter, the king of the gods. Below them are Mars, the god of war, and Mercury, the gods messenger, and Venus, the goddess of love.

The major powers in the region at that time were Greece and Carthage. Greece was engaged in fighting back the invading Persian empire, while Carthage was more interested in its trading empire in the western Mediterranean than in what was happening in Italy. As a result, the Roman Republic was able to grow in size and power without much interference from outside.

Conquest

After Rome defeated the neighbouring Latins in battle in 496 BC, the two sides agreed in a series of treaties to fight together against outsiders. However, Rome was still unable to hold back the Celts when they surged into central Italy in 386 BC. The city was overpowered and, although the Celts were driven out, it was 50 years before Rome became dominant once more. The Romans strengthened their army in 434 BC and set out to conquer more land. By 264 BC the whole of Italy was under their control.

As they began to expand still further, the Romans came into conflict with Carthage. During the First Punic War (264-241 BC) Rome captured Sicily, and then went on to take Corsica and Sardinia. In the Second Punic War (218-201 BC), despite the bravery of Hannibal and his army (see pages 52-53), Spain was seized from Carthage.

The Republic then looked eastwards for new territories. Macedonia, Syria, Cilicia, Cyprus, and Crete all fell under Roman domination by 58 BC. In Africa, Cyrene and Carthage were defeated, while in Europe Rome captured all of what is now France. By 44 BC the entire Mediterranean world was under Roman control.

Roman Society

When the Roman Republic was first set up it was ruled by a group of long-established families, known as the patricians, and the ordinary citizens, or plebeians, had very little power. The slaves, who were far below even the plebeians on the social scale, had no power at all. The wealthy patricians lived in great luxury, with their slaves to do the work for them, both in their houses in the city and at their villas and farms in the country. Outside Rome, some provincial governors forced their subjects to pay huge taxes.

Over the years, the plebeians managed to take away some of the patricians' rights, but this was not enough to prevent the civil war that broke out during the first century BC. This was caused by two Roman generals who were both trying to seize more power. Then, in 73 BC, a slave called Spartacus led a revolt of 90,000 other slaves. The final blow to the Roman Republic came when two of the most important army generals, Julius Caesar and Pompey, fought each other for control of the government. In the end, Caesar triumphed and in about 48 BC he became the sole ruler, or dictator, of Rome.

THE ROMAN EMPIRE

Four years after he had gained control of Rome, Julius Caesar was murdered and the empire was plunged into civil war. Caesar's adopted son, Octavian, succeeded in leading his supporters to victory against Brutus and Cassius - two of Caesar's assassins - and then defeated his other rivals for power, Mark Antony and the Egyptian queen Cleopatra. In doing so he became the master of the empire, and brought it a period of stability that was to last for 250 years.

Imperial Power

In 27 BC Octavian became Rome's first emperor, and from then on he was known as Augustus. During his rule he set about changing the way in which the empire was run. He reduced the size of the army and stationed many of its soldiers on the frontiers; he gave most of the empire's population the right to govern themselves; and he enabled talented people from all parts of the empire to rise to some of the most important positions in the government.

Thanks to Augustus' reforms, the empire remained peaceful and was able to concentrate on expanding its borders. Around AD 117, under Trajan, it reached its greatest extent, and included England and Wales, all of Europe south of the River Rhine and River Danube, western Asia south of the Black Sea, Syria, Egypt, and north Africa. At that time it had a population of 50 to 60 million.

The empire's wealth came mainly from agriculture and trade. Food and other goods were traded throughout the Mediterranean and beyond - to Britain, northern Europe and as far east as India. Most trade went by sea as this was easier than transporting goods by land. The empire was crisscrossed by an impressive system of roads, but they were used mainly by people on official business and for the movement of soldiers.

Life in Imperial Rome

At the heart of the empire was the city of Rome itself, home to a million people. It was a city of open squares, called forums, and imposing buildings. There was the Circus Maximus where chariot racing and athletics contests were held, and the Colosseum where, on public holidays, 70,000 bloodthirsty spectators could watch men fighting each other to the death, or being killed by wild animals. After a

Below: A Roman soldier from about AD 100, and the equipment he had to carry.

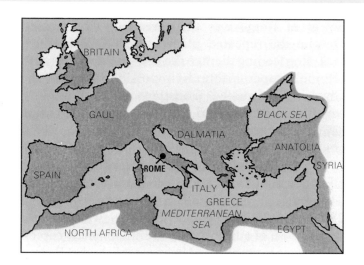

Above: The Roman empire at the time of Emperor Trajan in about AD 117.

Below: This large town house would have belonged to a wealthy Roman citizen.

morning's work Roman men could spend the afternoon at one of the many public baths; women went in the morning when men were not allowed in, or visited baths that were built especially for them. There were also markets, shops, temples, tombs built for past emperors, and, of course, houses.

Wealthy Roman families lived in large comfortable houses consisting of a number of rooms built around a courtyard, or *atrium*. There would be a kitchen, dining room, storerooms, bedrooms, servants' rooms, and a special room where guests were entertained. Some houses had lavatories that led into drains below, and some even had a hypocaust, a system of central heating in the form of hot air that flowed underneath the stone floors. The cooking, cleaning, and other household duties were all carried out by slaves.

The houses of poor people were very different. Most Romans lived in blocks of flats called *insulae*; when there was a shortage of housing, more flats were built on top of the blocks. Because of the risk of fire, people were not allowed to have cooking stoves above the ground floor. There were plenty of take-away shops where food could be bought and either eaten at once or taken home.

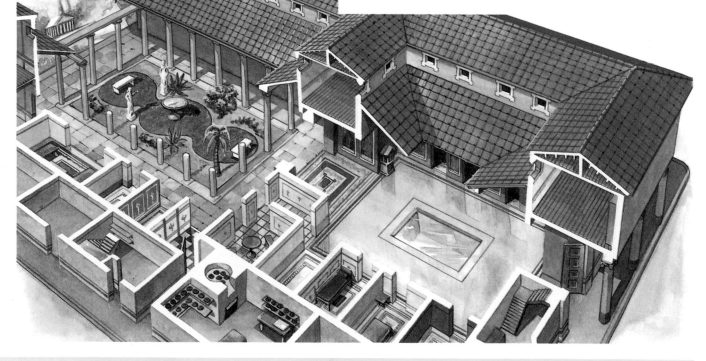

ROMAN EMPIRE AT ITS LARGEST c.AD 117 • POPULATION 50-60 MILLION

JAPAN AND KOREA

Until about 1500 BC the people of Korea and Japan lived mainly by fishing, gathering plants from the wild, and growing vegetables. One of the major changes to their way of life came when rice and millet were introduced, first to Korea and then to western Japan about 1000 years later.

Korea

These crops were brought to Korea from China. At first, the people of northern Korea grew mainly millet and soya beans, while those in the south cultivated rice, but later on rice-growing spread throughout the country.

The art of making bronze ornaments and weapons was also introduced to Korea from Manchuria, to the north of China, in around 1000 BC. Early Korean bronze mirrors and daggers are very like those that were made in Manchuria, but gradually Korean craftsmen developed styles of their own. Only the wealthiest people could afford bronze, and from the objects found in Korean tombs it seems that most of these rich people lived in the south of the country; very few northern tombs contain bronzes. Bronze was not used to make everyday items: farmers continued to use tools which were made from stone and wood.

The Han dynasty of China took control of Korea in 108 BC, but as they fell into decline from around AD 200, they were replaced by new groups. The first major civilizations that grew up in Korea were called the Shilla, Paekche, and Koguryo. The strongest of these was the Shilla, which spread outwards from its base in the south-east and, by AD 668, had managed to unite the entire country.

Japan

The early people of Japan, known as the Jomon, depended heavily on fishing. However, when rice-growing first appeared on the western island of Kyushu in around 500 BC, a new culture developed, called the Yayoi. Like their predecessors in Korea, Yayoi farmers used wooden hoes and spades, and stone knives for cutting the seed heads from the rice plants. When the rice had been harvested, it was stored in special granaries that were built on stilts to keep it off the ground and so dry and protected from rats and mice.

Below: The early states which grew up in Korea and Japan before AD 300.

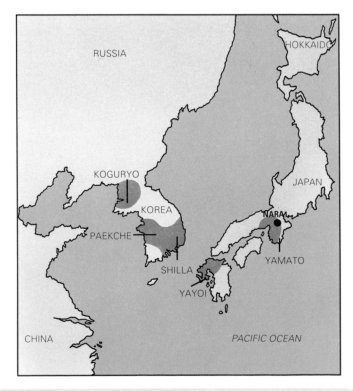

By AD 300 rice-growing had spread throughout the whole of Japan, apart from the island of Hokkaido in the far north. Also at that time Japan's first powerful state - the Yamato - developed in central Honshu. Yamato rulers were buried in huge tombs shaped like keyholes. The largest tomb that has been found belonged to the emperor Nintoku, who died in about AD 475. It covers a huge area, 475 m by 200 m, and is surrounded by three water-filled moats. Around it are smaller tombs built for nobles. Buddhism reached Japan from China in around AD 550, and temples were then built instead of tombs.

As the Yamato state became stronger and started to expand northwards, it came into conflict with the local populations it tried to control. On Hokkaido, the local people built a large number of hill-forts to defend themselves. By 700, however, most of Japan was under Yamato control. In AD 710 the Yamato state gave way to a new, unified Japanese state with its capital at Nara.

Left: A Yayoi rice granary.

Below: Emperor Nintoku's keyhole tomb.

RISE OF YAMATO STATE c.AD 300 • **BUDDHISM REACHES JAPAN FROM CHINA** c.AD 550

AFTER ALEXANDER

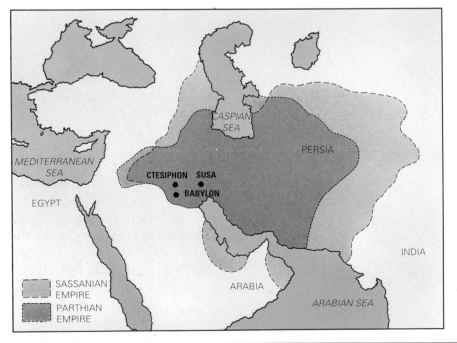

Above: The city of Ctesiphon, beside the River Euphrates, became the Parthian capital in the first century BC and was taken over by the Sassanians 400 years later.

Left: When the Seleucid empire was broken up after 192 BC, part of it was taken over by the Parthians. Their empire fell to the Sassanians in AD 226.

Right: This silver-gilt dish shows King Ardashir III, who ruled from AD 628 to 630, near the end of the Sassanian empire. Hunting was a favourite royal pastime.

SELEUCID EMPIRE RULES PERSIA 312-192 BC • PARTHIAN EMPIRE 171 BC-AD 226

Following the death of Alexander the Great, the Persian part of the Macedonian empire was taken over by Seleucus in 312 BC. Almost immediately he was faced with rebellions and attacks from outside his empire. Early in his reign he was forced to give up the area around the River Indus to the increasingly powerful Mauryans, and under later Seleucid rulers, Syria and other lands were lost. Finally, in 192 BC, the armies of Republican Rome crushed the Seleucids and the empire broke up into a number of independent kingdoms and provinces.

The Parthians

Among these kingdoms was Parthia, a land to the south-east of the Caspian Sea. From 171 BC it was ruled by Mithridates, who conquered Babylonia and transformed the Parthians into the major power in the region.

The Parthians were, however, surrounded by enemies. When Mithridates II extended his empire westwards to the River Euphrates, he came up against the Romans; in the east, attacks by the Kushans and Scythians kept Parthian troops on the defensive. There was also rebellion within the empire itself. Through frequent intrigues and murders, a succession of rulers took the Parthian throne.

This weakened the empire and gave Rome an excuse to intervene. At first, the Romans simply supported one or another of the rival claimants to the Parthian throne. But finally, the Roman emperor Trajan invaded Parthia.

The Romans' influence was short-lived, but Parthia was soon threatened from other directions and the empire steadily shrank in size. Eventually, the Sassanian kingdom of Iran broke what little power the Parthians had.

The Sassanian Empire

Under the Sassanian king Ardashir a new kingdom of Iran was founded after the defeat of the Parthians in AD 226. His son, Shapur I, expanded the kingdom to include all of modern Iran and parts of what are now Afghanistan, Pakistan, the USSR, Iraq, and the Gulf coast of Arabia. As had happened before, the growing empire attracted the attention of the Romans, who tried and failed to defeat the Sassanians in AD 244.

A few years later, Shapur decided to go on the offensive and he conquered Syria. Again the Romans attacked, launching a disastrous assault in which their emperor, Valerian, was captured. In the east, Shapur added the territory of the Kushans to his growing empire.

Shapur died in 276, and during the 30 years that followed, his successors lost nearly all of the lands he had gained. But out of the chaos there emerged a new leader, Shapur II, who became one of the strongest rulers in Sassanian history. He recovered the lost territories and, after brief skirmishes with the Romans, captured the province of Armenia.

Following the death of Shapur II in 339, two new threats faced the Sassanian empire. One of these was the nobles within the empire, who were becoming increasingly powerful. The other came from nomadic tribes, called the Hepthalites, beyond the north-eastern border. In 484 the Sassanian King Peroz was killed in battle and from then on the Sassanians were dominated by the Hepthalites. They recovered some of their former glory under Khusrao I (531-579), but between 633 and 642 the empire was conquered by the Arabs - followers of the Muslim prophet Muhammad.

THE KUSHANS

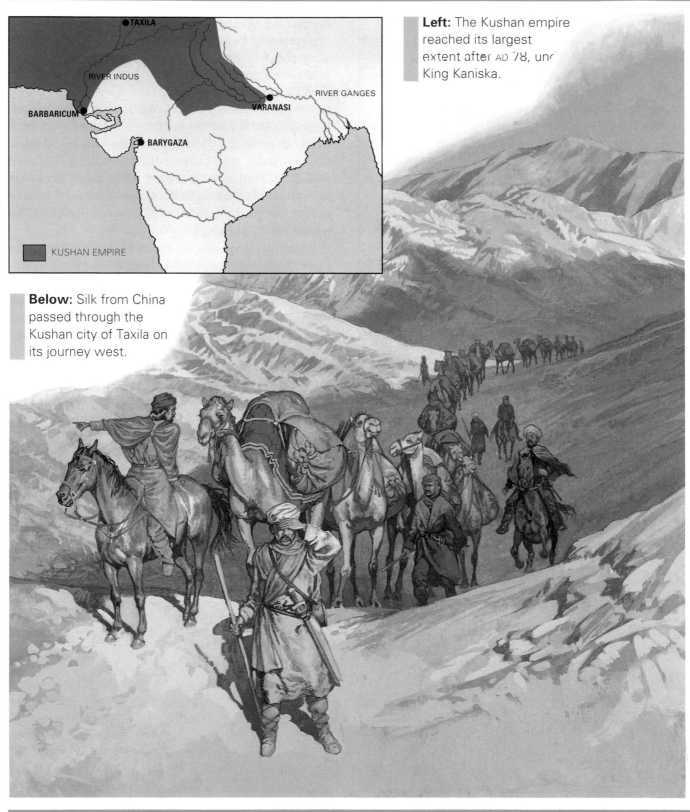

Left: The Kushan empire reached its largest extent after AD 78, under King Kaniska.

TAXILA

RIVER INDUS

RIVER GANGES

BARBARICUM

VARANASI

BARYGAZA

KUSHAN EMPIRE

Below: Silk from China passed through the Kushan city of Taxila on its journey west.

YUEH-CHIH SETTLE IN CENTRAL ASIA c.165 BC • KANISKA BECOMES KING AD 78

Above: A statue from Taxila of the Buddha, carved in the Gandharan style.

The history of the Kushan empire of India has its beginnings in China. When China's first emperor, Shih Huang-ti, united his country in 221 BC, the nomadic tribes who lived in the pasturelands on the western borders were driven out. These tribes, the Hsiung-nu and Yueh-chih, were forced to move into central Asia.

The Yueh-chih settled in the valley of the River Oxus in about 165 BC. They did not immediately spread into India, mainly because they were not a united tribe but were split into five separate groups. Eventually one of these groups, the Kushans, defeated the other four and began a period of conquest.

The Kushans in India

The first Kushan ruler, Kadphises I, extended his territories to the Indus Valley. He was succeeded by Kadphises II, who conquered most of the area known as the Punjab. The third and most powerful king, Kaniska, came to the throne in about AD 78. During his reign he gained control of an empire that stretched from Varanasi in the River Ganges valley to deep inside central Asia.

Within the empire there was a wide range of different cultures, including Indian, Chinese, central Asian, Greek, and Roman. This was reflected in the art which was produced; for example, the sculptures of Gandhara in north-west India are a mixture of Indian and Greek styles.

India had trade links with the Middle East and Egypt dating from centuries earlier. During the time of the Kushan empire, and especially under Kaniska, these links were strengthened and new ones added. By the first century AD the Roman historian Pliny recorded that Indian spices, jewels, textiles, and exotic animals were being imported by the Roman empire. Spice traders in the Kushan empire, eager to satisfy the demand of their customers overseas, travelled throughout South-East Asia buying local spices. For a time, a great deal of the Chinese silk trade passed through the Indian city of Taxila on its way westwards. Indian ports such as Barbaricum on the delta of the River Indus and Barygaza near the mouth of the River Narmada, were shipping cargoes of diamonds, turquoise, indigo, tortoise-shell, and silk. In return copper, pearls, wine, gold, slaves, and dates were imported from the Mediterranean region, Arabia, and Ethiopia.

The Kushan empire was at its height when the Romans were at their most powerful. Because of the Kushans' position between east and west, aspects of Western culture passed through them into India and beyond. The Kushans also helped to spread the teachings of Buddhism throughout their empire and into China.

The Decline of the Kushans

After Kaniska died in about 100 AD the Kushans' power began to fade in the Ganges valley. In the third century AD they came up against the new Sassanian rulers of Persia, and other parts of their empire were taken by invading nomadic tribes. From this time onwards, the Kushan dynasty never again played an important part in the affairs of Asia.

KANISKA DIES c.100 AD • KUSHAN EMPIRE FADES IN THIRD CENTURY AD

THE GUPTA EMPIRE

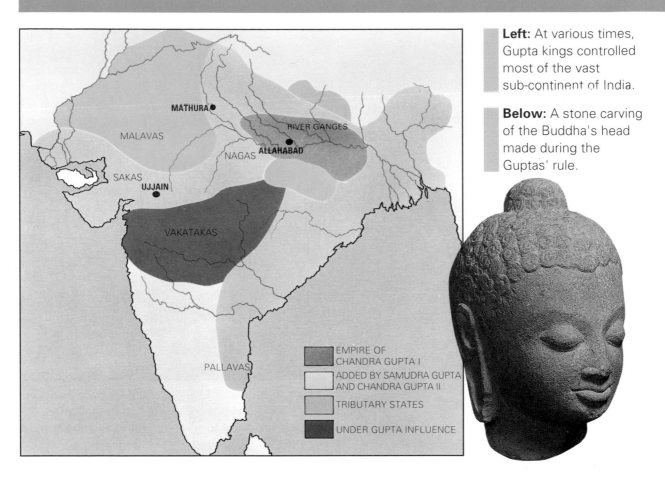

Left: At various times, Gupta kings controlled most of the vast sub-continent of India.

Below: A stone carving of the Buddha's head made during the Guptas' rule.

EMPIRE OF CHANDRA GUPTA I

ADDED BY SAMUDRA GUPTA AND CHANDRA GUPTA II

TRIBUTARY STATES

UNDER GUPTA INFLUENCE

During the fourth century AD a new dynasty appeared in the Ganges valley of India, in the area known as Magadha. At first the Gupta kingdom was simply one among many in the region, but in 320 its new ruler, Chandra Gupta I, began to expand his power. During his 15-year reign he gained control over the whole Ganges valley, from Allahabad in the west to the borders of Bengal in the east.

A Growing Empire

When Chandra Gupta died in 335 his son Samudra Gupta came to the throne. He used the empire which his father had created as a base from which to conquer more territory. He led an expedition into south India and reached Kanchi, the capital of a dynasty called the Pallavas. On the way he subdued many smaller kingdoms and forced them to pay him tribute (money or valuable goods) to show their allegiance to him. The wealth he gained in this way was used to pay for other campaigns in the north of

India. He was so successful that by the time of his death in 376 only one other independent kingdom of any size remained in the northern part of India - that of the Sakas.

Samudra was followed by Chandra Gupta II, his son, who became the most powerful of all Gupta rulers. He went a step further than his father and conquered the Sakas; he may also have used their capital, Ujjain, as his own headquarters. By marrying a member of the Vakataka dynasty in central India, he also became the overlord of that kingdom, although only for a short time.

It has been said that during Chandra Gupta II's reign India was the most civilized country in the world; in the west the Roman Empire was under attack from the barbarians, and China was also in crisis. Chandra Gupta II was certainly a highly civilized ruler, and his name is linked with the finest writers of the time, such as the poet Kalidasa.

EXPANSION OF GUPTA EMPIRE 320-414 • PEACE UNDER KUMARA GUPTA 414-454

Above: This Buddhist temple was carved out of the rocks at Ellora, western India.

Above: Part of a fifth-century Bodhisattva (divine being) carved in the Gupta style.

The Hepthalites

The empire continued to thrive under its next ruler, Kumara Gupta. During most of his reign, from 414 to 454, northern India was peaceful and prosperous, and the arts continued to flourish; some of the finest Indian painting to have survived was done during this time.

Towards the end of Kumara's rule, after a period of expansion which had lasted over 100 years, the fortunes of the Guptas began to change. A nomadic group called the Hepthalites, or White Huns, had seized parts of central Asia and Afghanistan in the fourth century, and in the middle of the fifth century they captured most of the Punjab. In around 450 the Guptas came under direct attack and their power was shaken. Kumara died during this war and his place was taken by his son, Skanda Gupta. The new ruler managed to fight off the Hepthalites, but soon afterwards other threats appeared.

Beyond the Ganges plain - the heartland of the Gupta empire - provincial governors were beginning to set themselves up as kings, ignoring the power of the Gupta rulers. Gradually the empire shrank to the size it had been under Chandra Gupta I. Furthermore, the Hepthalites once again turned their attentions towards India, and in 500 they attacked in force. Although they were eventually pushed back to Kashmir in the north-west, the Hepthalites damaged the Guptas' power beyond repair. Countless new kingdoms sprang up, taking advantage of the Guptas' weakness. The empire survived in some parts of north-east India until about 650, but it was an empire in name only.

FIRST ATTACKS BY HEPTHALITES c.450 • GUPTA EMPIRE GROWS WEAKER FROM c.475

INDEX

ACKNOWLEDGEMENTS

The publishers would like to thank the following organizations and individuals for their kind permission to reproduce the pictures in this book:

Ancient Art & Architecture/R. Sheridan 9, 19, 30, 43, 77; Michael Holford 10, 12, 17, 24, 35, 40, 54, 66, 76, 77; Robert Harding Picture Library 11, 15, 23, 36-37, 41, 46, 47, 48, 51, 67, 68 front cover centre; C. M. Dixon 15, 21, 26, 27, 30, 33, 57, 63, 69; Cambridge University Library 16; Sonia Halliday 28, 35, 46, 53; Werner Forman 36; Aerofilms 39; Mansell Collection 63; Magnum/ I. Morath 71; Peter Newark Pictures 75; Douglas Dickins 73; Georg Gerster 65; Hutchison Library front cover left.

Illustrations by:

Richard Berridge (Specs Art Agency) - pages 12 - 13, 14-15, 19, 26 - 27, 30 - 31, 52 - 53, 54 - 55, 57, 59, 70 - 71, 72
Wayne Ford - page 7
Finbarr O'Connor - pages 11, 16, 20 - 21, 23 right, 24-25, 29, 38 - 39, 42, 44, 60, 62
The Maltings Partnership - pages 8, 22 - 23, 33, 61, 74
Mark Stacey - pages 6, 7, 34 - 35, 45, 49, 58, 64 -65, pull-out time chart

Illustrations in top right-hand corners by Joe Lawrence

All maps plus page 24 inset by Peter Bull Art Studios

The illustrations in the top right-hand corners of the right hand pages in this book show the following:

Page 7, Altamira cave painting; page 9, wheat and barley; page 11, 'Ram in Thicket' from Sumer; page 13, Egyptian wall painting; page 15, statue of a god or priest-king from Mohenjo-Daro; page 17, Shang jade spearhead; page 19, statue of Anubis from Tutankhamun's tomb; page 21, stag shield centrepiece from Scythian tomb; page 23, early navigation chart; page 25, Minoan double-headed axe; page 27, bull's head from Babylon, page 29, Hittite chariot; page 31, lion gate at Mycenae; page 33, Phoenician bust; page 35, the Ark of the Covenant; page 37, Olmec stone head; page 39 Celtic brooch; page 41, Etruscan terracotta head of warrior; page 43, Assyrian siege machine; page 45, Greek vase; page 47, funerary statuette from Qataban; page 49, Nok head; page 51, Persian gold armlet from Oxus treasure; page 53, statuette of Carthaginian warrior; page 55, bronze voting disks; page 57, cameo of Alexander the Great and his wife Roxanne; page 59, she-wolf symbolising Rome's greatness; page 61, SPQR symbol of Rome; page 63, head of Constantine the Great; page 65, statuette of Japanese warrior; page 67, the Buddhist Stupa at Sanchi; page 69, Sassanian relief; page 71, Chinese lacquer bowl; page 73, Kushan statue of a tree spirit; page 75, North American decoy duck from Nevada; page 77, Chandra Gupta I and his queen on gold coin